CREATING A NEW YOU

CREATING A NEW YOU

LEONARD PRATHER

AUCTOREM
HOUSE

Auctorem House
276 5th Ave, Ste 704-2591
New York, NY 10001
www.auctoremhouse.com
Phone: 1 888-332-7718

Published by Auctorem House: 05/22/2025

ISBN: 978-1-965687-76-5(sc)
ISBN: 978-1-965687-77-2(e)

Library of Congress Control Number: 2025900906

Contents

Preface

In the beginning was the Word, and the
Word was with God, and the Word was God
(John 1:1).

Life is a journey to be embraced one day at a time. In life, we don't have all the answers. And, we definitely will not always know what to do, what to say, how to face adversity, or how to rebuild our lives after a devastating event. If we live solely by our own desires and influences of the world around us, we often find ourselves constrained. Our success, abilities, resources, and opportunities are left to our natural and physical limitations. While this may bring us some sense of contentment or satisfaction, and achievement, it begs the question: are you truly happy?

Creating a New You! is a discovery into the art of living a fulfilling life personally, professionally, socially, and spiritually. It emphasizes the importance of making wise decisions, setting positive goals, cultivating relationships, and maintaining an active relationship with God. The book outlines practical advice for managing temptations, coping with adversity, building self-discipline, and developing resilience. And, encourages the reader to embrace a journey of personal growth, find purpose, and live one day at a time with intention and faith.

By embracing personal growth, there's no limit to what you can accomplish—or the happiness you can experience.

There is an art to living! Experience the journey of living a fulfilling life and get started *"Creating a New You!"*

Today

*In the beginning God created the heaven
and the earth. And God called the light Day,
and the darkness he called Night. And the
evening and the morning were the first day
(Gen. 1:1 and 1:5).*

Today is a new day.
A chance to start over.
A new beginning.
A fresh start!

Today is a gift. A precious gift wrapped in the present called today! Live one day at a time, one moment at time, making the most of each day. Yesterday is past. Tomorrow is not promised. And, the future? Starts now!

Life

In him was life; and "the life was the light of men" (John 1:4).

L - Live.

I - Invest.

F - Form healthy relationships.

E - Encourage Godly Living.

Live.

Live one day at a time.

Make the most of each day.

Strive to do your best.

Appreciate what you have.

Welcome the good times and hardships.

Invest.

Invest in yourself and others.

Work with all your heart and soul.

Form relationships.

Love yourself and others.

Encourage Godly Living.

Have respect for GOD and obey Him.

Temptation!

And, lead us not into temptation, but
deliver us from evil: (Matt. 6:13)

Throughout our life, we encounter temptation. It roams about looking for someone vulnerable to influence. The thesaurus describes temptation as - lure, entice, seduce, invite, captivate, appeal to, attract, persuade or urge. Webster defines temptation as to "entice to do wrong by promise of pleasure or gain". According to Webster, thesaurus, and scripture temptation is a way of influencing us to do wrong. No good ever comes from giving into temptation. Its benefits are short lived. And, eventually, when our wrong doing is exposed our demise begins.

So many lives have been ruined because of temptation. Unfortunately, society is saturated with it. As man becomes more educated and moves away from his spiritual roots and God, we become more susceptible to the influences of temptation and wrong doing. What use to be forbidden, is now normal. Over the past years, there has been an increase in crime, corruption, and murder. The entertainment industry has increased its focus on drama by incorporating themes of sex, scandal, murder, poltergeists, and paranormal activity into its programming. Television and radio is now free to use improper language. And, some television advertising is borderline inappropriate. The music industry has begun using explicit language in their lyrics. Christian music is becoming more commercial and less spiritual. Although, these forms of programming are meant to entertain and inform. They also influence our thoughts and behavior. Even, some of our spiritual leaders have fallen into temptation and worldly influences.

Society as we know it, is changing. Temptation is becoming more and more prevalent. So, it's important you establish a relationship with God and move forward with a new vision and purpose. So, you can be strong and encouraged to resist temptation.

Come What May ...

The Lord is my shepherd (Ps. 23).

Whatever comes my way
I may be concerned
But, I need not worry.
Because, the Lord helps me through it.
He and His Staff comfort me.
And, leads me to the truth.
He helps me find peace.
I acknowledge His presence and
Works on my behalf.
Surely, His goodness and mercy
Follows me.
Because, my blessings overflow.
Come what may,
The Lord is my help!

Each day we're faced with numerous decisions and situations beyond our control, we may not always know what to say, how to react, or what to do during those moments. But, we do have an inner voice that speaks to us through the arousal of our inner being and consciousness. The inner voice is like a tap on the shoulder trying to get our attention and help us make the right choice, say the right thing, and react in the right way. When our natural being (intellect, emotions, and senses) is busy reacting to the natural world and deciding what to do, our inner voice is aroused to help. If we train ourselves to listen and obey our inner voice, we'll be able to face what comes our way.

A Repeat Course!

Wisdom is the principal thing; therefore get wisdom:
and with all thy getting get understanding....
(Prov. 4:7)

Have you ever felt like you're faced with the same situation over and over, like a repeat course?

It's almost impossible to learn from every mistake or wrong decision. Things happen and having the right attitude is key to overcoming obstacles and making the right choice. Human nature also plays a role in influencing our thoughts and decisions. And, it's a guarantee our circumstances will not always cooperate. However, we can minimize our conflicts and influences by taking the time to learn from our mistakes and circumstances.

Whatever the reason for your situation, be trained by it. Learn from it and master it. Take one day at a time. Ask for God's help. Make whatever changes are necessary. Do what is required of you. And, let time take its course. Endure without murmuring, grumbling or complaining. Be encouraged, knowing and believing God is providing, helping, and enabling you along the way. By doing so, you'll become wiser and able to handle similar situations as life goes on.

Otherwise, you'll find yourself in the same situation like a repeat course!

What have I learned?

Those things, which ye have both learned,
and received, and heard, and seen in me, do:
and the God of peace shall be with you....
(Phil. 4:9)

We're all faced with situations from time to time beyond our control. It's part of life. Sometimes the situations we face come from the decisions of others, our decisions, negative influences, associations and places we go. Things we hear, see and read all effect our ability to make decisions. Learning the hard way can create some painful lessons from which we can learn. But, it's not recommended we learn the hard way.

If you want life to go well, you must be willing to accept sound advice, change your way of thinking and behavior, be willing to learn from your decisions and the decisions of others who affect you, learn to adapt and have a positive attitude is essential to living a good life. Of course, this isn't easy. It takes time! The more you put into practice these principles, you'll see a transformation in your way of thinking and behaving.

More often than not, life is out of our control. You can't control the behavior of others. But you can control your behavior, what you say, do and think. When interacting with others, be mindful what you say and how you say it. It can affect them in a positive or negative way. When your actions don't align with your words, it can create confusion.

When it comes to those you care about and want to help, you

can only suggest and hope they'll listen. There are many reasons why people find it hard to change and listen to sound advice. Some don't want to change. Some are creatures of habit, which are hard to change. Some are influenced by others, who may have a significant impact on their behavior and or way of life. Others have their own agenda and only care about what they want. These individuals may not be open to advice or counsel. So they aren't too concerned what others thinks. Or, how their actions or decisions affects others.

In some cases, you may be affected by another in a negative way. If possible try and talk to them about it. Work it out. You may be surprised to find cooperation and support when you decide to include them in the decision making process. If, however, they're not receptive or willing to listen. Then, let it go, put it behind you and move on. Like it or not, you must be willing to accept their decision and decide how to handle it.

Although, we have some control over our own life. There are time when the actions of others have a direct or indirect impact on your life and how you view it. Not every day, is going to go well. Human nature will be arouse at times and play a role in how you perceive things. The moment you decide to make an important decision, doubt and emotion will come into play to test your decision.

Life's a journey, be trained by it. Be careful who you associate with, monitor what feeds your senses, and beware who and what influences you. Make whatever changes are necessary. Adjust your attitude. Change your way of thinking and think it through. Get advice. And, let time take its course. By doing so, what you have learned?

It's Your Choice!

Hear instruction, and be wise, and refuse it not.
(Prov. 8:33)

Sometimes, the only voice you hear is yours and not the voice of others. Whether you ask or not, your parents, loved ones, and those who care about you will try to offer advice when they think you need it. But, you're not always willing to listen to what they have to say or accept their advice. So you ignore it, create distractions, change the subject, get angry, and dismiss it.

If you want to enjoy life, achieve your goals, be happy and content, face life's challenges, and aspire to achieve, you must be willing to accept correction and advice from others. You may not always agree with what he or she has to say. But, if you talk it out, you'll certainly gain something from it. You can learn something from anyone, anybody, at any time if you're open to it.

When you choose to follow sound advice, God will help you carry out your decision. If you choose to follow a different path, He'll step aside and let you have your way. He will not interfere and support a wrong decision. He'll wait patiently until you ask for His help. Then, God will kindly lead you to the right decision.

If you're unsure how to solve a problem, ask God to get involved in your decision making process, He could send a friend, parent, stranger or anyone He chooses to get His message across. Or,

He may choose to speak to you directly providing insight and answers to what you need or want to know. God knows how to communicate with us when we need it. All you have to do is be willing to listen and obey. The choice is yours!

A Walk with God!

*Ye shall walk in all the ways which the Lord your God
hath commanded you, that ye may live, and that
it may be well with you, and that ye may prolong
your days in the land which ye shall possess.*
(Deut. 5:33)

To walk with God means to conduct yourself in accordance with His teachings and principles and allow Him to be an active part of your life. God teaches us in many ways. He teaches us through the Bible. The Bible contains principles of daily living that can be achieved by anyone who reads the Bible and puts into practice its teachings and principles. God teaches us through others to guide and correct us. God speaks to us directly through the arousal of our inner being or voice. Sometimes, we ignore His guidance, teachings and correction. And, follow our own thoughts and desires.

When we establish a relationship with God and allow Him to guide us, we can learn to make the right choices, accept correction, exercise self-control, and develop a willingness to put into practice the insight given us regarding our health, finances, relationships, profession, future and more.

God wants to be involved in your life. And by walking with God, you can live a more fulfilling life and experience His presence!

A Faith Walk

When the disciples saw it, they marveled,
saying, How soon the fig tree withered away!
Jesus answered and said unto them, Verily I
say unto you, If ye have faith, and doubt not,
ye shall not only do this which is done, but
also if ye say unto this mountain, Be removed,
and cast into the sea; and it shall be done
(Matt. 21:20–21).

Work at what you believe.
Believe in what you are doing.
Believing alone is not enough.
Belief must be accompanied by work.
And, must not waver when tested.
The testing produces endurance.
Be patient
Allowing time for your faith and work to produce.
So, you may accomplish what you believe.
And, be filled with joy!

When you walk with God, it means you're putting your faith in Him. Likewise, a faith walk means believing and trusting in God. God can speak to you through the Bible, through others and directly to you. If you train yourself to recognize and obey these levels of communication, you can achieve your full potential.

God wants you to be happy and live a fulfilling life. But, you must be willing to apply yourselves, accept correction, exercise discipline and self-control, and put into practice the insight given to you. Without this leadership, you can be misguided and lead astray. If you believe in yourself, trust in God, learn to follow sound advice, and work at what you believe, you can achieve your full potential. And, live a fulfilling life!

I Have a Dream!

By works faith is made perfect (James 2:22).

I have a dream placed in my heart.
I pursue it with a love for it.
I work at it day and night.
Making it a part of who I am.
So, that I know without a doubt.
This is what I was born to do!

When you know in your heart what you aspire to achieve or want out of life, your whole being becomes consumed by it. Your will, your intellect, and emotions all urge and encourage you to get started learning, growing, and fulfilling your aspiration. Pursuing your aspirations requires sacrifice, discipline, self-control, education, and experience in areas of interest. Be patient and commit yourself to the task day and night, making it a part of who you are. So, that you know without a doubt this is what you were born to do!

The Possibilities are endless!

And he said, The things which are impossible
with men are possible with God
(Luke 18:27).

Imagine life without boundaries!

Soaring with the angels.

Living, loving and enjoying life.

We are all capable of achieving endless possibilities for our life. Whether you aspire to achieve great things or want to live a simple life, if you change your way of thinking and not let your circumstances dictate your joy or happiness, you can live and enjoy life.

With the right attitude, you can turn an unfortunate situation or event into a positive lesson or outcome.

There are some things you have no control over. The action or decision of another, or your own decisions can change your life. Those moments can be managed if you learn to walk with the counsel of God!

Whether we ask or not, there are times when God will intervene and helps us in our time of need. All of us receive God's counsel to help us make the right decision and face what comes our way. God knows how to communicate with us when He wants to guide, counsel and correct us. It can be the arousal of our inner being or someone God has sent to speak on His behalf. It's up to you to recognize and obey His voice when He speaks.

So, you can live, love and enjoy the endless possibilities of life!

You Can Do It!

I can do all things through Christ who strengthens me
(Phil. 4:13).

Faith alone is not enough.
Faith must be accompanied by work.
Your work must be accompanied by action.
Your action must be accompanied by faith.
Your faith will be tested.
The testing produces endurance.
Endurance supports your faith.
Through faith you will be made whole.
And lack nothing!

Whatever you put your mind to, you can accomplish. Remain faithful to your commitment to excel and aspire to achieve. There's no easy formula for success. Success is accomplished when you commit yourself to the task, make sacrifices, and find ways to work it out without getting distracted, fall off course, or decide to postpone or abandon your plans. Your commitment will be tested and will require you to balance your ambitions with personal responsibilities.

Human nature will also play a role as you pursue your ambition. You'll feel guilty and influenced to spend more time with those you care about. But, you must learn to manage your time while concentrating on what needs to be done.

Your emotions will run high and try to influence you. So, it's important to keep your emotions in check. Unexpected circumstances and influences will attack your weaknesses and make you feel vulnerable, guilty and pressured. When you're vulnerable, it can interfere with your ability to concentrate and accomplish what needs to be done. Accomplishment requires commitment and sacrifice. So when you're attacked, it points out areas of vulnerability that need strengthening.

Be obedient to your commitment and put into practice the insights given you regarding what is required. Learn how to handle distractions, manage hardship, adversity, and stress. Remain faithful. Be patient. Work it out. And, work at it. Accept trials as a test to your commitment. Commitment produces endurance. Endurance will support your faith and help you accomplish your goal!

What's Life All About?

And 'God saw everything that he had made,
and behold, it was very good. And, the evening
and the morning were the sixth day.
(Gen. 1:31)

Throughout the Bible and history, we learn we are blessed with exceptional talent and abilities from God. If you read any newspaper, watch reality shows, observe TV commercials, follow the careers of actors, millionaires, and billionaires, you can see the great talent we possess. So, I encourage you to take control of your life and start adding purpose to it. And, you will see how great you can be! Remember success is not measured by wealth. Not everyone wants to be wealthy. A simple life can be just as rewarding. A good life is rooted in a relationship with God in our daily living experience personally, professionally, socially, and spiritually. When achieved, it's truly "A Blessed Life!"

If you change your way of thinking and don't let your circumstances or people dictate your joy or happiness, you can live and enjoy life. With the right attitude, you can turn an unfortunate situation or event into a positive lesson or outcome.

There are some things you have no control over. Those moments can be managed if you learn to walk with the counsel of God. All of us receive God's counsel to help us make the right decision and face what comes our way. God knows how to communicate with us when He wants to guide, counsel, and correct us. It's up to you to recognize and obey His voice when He speaks. Learn to recognize the voice of God. It can be a parent, friend, or complete stranger trying to communicate with you in a profound way that gives you honest counsel when needed. Sometimes, God will speak to you directly by arousing your instincts, intellect, and inner being. Learn to recognize and accept this way of counsel and support, so you can live, love, and enjoy life.

Remain faithful to your commitment to change and live a good life. There's no easy formula for success. Success is accomplished when you commit yourself to the task, make sacrifices, and find ways TO work it out, without getting distracted, fall off course, or decide to postpone or abandon your plans.

Your commitment will be tested and will require you to balance your ambitions with personal responsibilities and general influences. Human nature and emotions will try to influence your thoughts, creating doubt and distraction. The unexpected and outside influences will attack your weaknesses causing you to feel vulnerable, guilty, and pressured. When vulnerable, it can interfere with your ability to concentrate and accomplish what needs to be done. These attacks point out areas of vulnerability that need strengthening.

Accomplishment requires commitment, sacrifice, and your undivided attention. Be obedient to your commitment and put into practice the insights given you regarding what is required. Learn how to handle distractions and manage hardship, adversity, and stress. Remain faithful. Be patient. Work at it. Accept trials as a test to your commitment. Commitment produces endurance. Endurance will support your faith and help you aspire to achieve.

Allow yourself to be a positive influence and role model to those you meet. Be a person, people can respect, trust, and look to for guidance and encouragement, if needed. Turn to God to help you manage worldly influences and its effect on you.

These spiritual essentials give us character and allows God to work through us, in us, and with us, giving us hope and renewing who we are. Those who learn to balance their spiritual self (inner being) and human nature will live in harmony with man, God and the world. Emulating what it means to be successful.

Things will not always go well. But, we have an unconditional support system (God) that can help us turn it around. When things are going well, we're happy and have a peace of mind and a clear perception to make the right decisions and manage the daily challenges we face. We as people should be constantly evolving into the person we were born to be. In this way, the Spirit of God can commune with you and transform you into the person you were created to be - Blessed!

Don't Give Up!

I press toward the mark for the prize
(Phil. 3:14).

I shall not be moved!
I will press toward the prize that waits.

I know I will be tested and faced with difficulties.
Each day will not always go as planned.
Some days, I will accomplish more than others.
But I shall not be moved.
I will press on remaining patient and
calm while working things out.

I will rid myself of old habits,
hindering thoughts,
and people who stand in the way of my progress.
I will free myself of strongholds that imprison me,
hold me back, wear me down,
and drain my energy so I give up.
I will stand my ground,
remain focused,
and run with determination toward the future that waits
with patience, discipline, and self-control.

Resting at times.
But not giving up!

We're all faced with situations from time to time that push
us to the limit. As you try to balance personal ambitions and

daily responsibilities self, others, and worldly influences will stir up trouble, attack your weaknesses, and create havoc on your emotions and intellect. You must learn to recognize these influences so you can manage them properly and not let them cause you to falter or give up. Take one day at a time. Accept the trials that come your way as a training ground to strengthen your vulnerabilities, apply yourself, develop the right attitude, and master the art of "access denied" to negative influences and distractions. Resting at times, but not giving up!

Now is the Time!

If you're wanting to start or renew your search for purpose, now is the time! Slow down, explore, and experience life. You can generate positive energy while searching for your purpose. Purpose exists when you found your interest. What interest you – personally, professionally, and socially? Do you have spiritual interest? What talents do you have to turn into a hobby or business? For example; if you enjoy cooking. Perhaps, you can turn that into a hobby or business. Share your favorite baked dish or treat with your family, friends, and associates and turn your interest into extra money. The new found purpose may renew your energy, change your perspective, and give you hope.

Use this week, to unwind, relax, reflect, and discover yourself. Reflect on personal values and passions, explore new perspectives, understand the challenges and opportunities you faced, envision the future, embrace curiosity, find inspiration in everyday, embrace faith or spirituality, engage with others to spark your imagination and inspiration. Call or visit a relative or friend you haven't spoken to or seen in a while. Enjoy some quiet time with family, friends, or yourself. Do something to help find that purpose in daily living that will inspire you to want to wake up each morning to get started.

Before you wind down tonight, prepare for tomorrow. What's

your to do list? What do you have planned? What needs to be accomplish or get done? What priorities do you have to complete today and tomorrow? Do you have any appointments or chores that need to be done? By planning ahead and getting things in order, you're setting yourself up for success. Preparing the night before will save you time the next day and add meaning and purpose to your day. Here are some suggestions how to add purpose to your daily living experience:

Family Time. Spend time with your family. Make it a habit of doing things together such as watching TV, playing games, make meal time family time to help foster a positive relationship with your family, friends, or loved one.

Meal time. Before you go to the grocery store, prepare a list of foods you will need to help you manage your budget and stay healthy.

Your time. Designate a quiet area in your home where you can focus on your thoughts, a task, and time with God. This will help you concentrate and increase efficiency.

Clean up. Perhaps, this is a good time to get organized. Start tossing out those items you no longer use, clean the garage, tidy up the basement, etc. Looking at a clean organized environment, can put a smile on your face.

Getting yourself organized, and creating some structure in your life can help you achieve some of the goals or ambitions you had in mind. Getting organized can improve productivity, reduce stress and anxiety, improve mental health, improve your work-life balance, build strong relationships, increase creativity, and improve sleep. Now is the time to do it!

Strength of the Human Spirit!

Be strong and of a good courage, fear not, nor be afraid of them: for the Lord thy God, he doth go with thee; he will not fail thee, nor forsake thee.
(Deut. 31.6)

Every day, we hear or read about human tragedies. These incredible stories reflect the strength and courage of the human spirit. For years, some individuals have endured torture, mental and physical abuse, wrongful imprisonment, and homeless. And, through it all, they maintained their sense of worth for survival to become successful or live a normal life. We may never get to experience, at least I hope not, what these men and women have gone through.

Everyday each of us are faced with the challenges of life resulting from our decisions and actions or the decisions and actions of others. Not every day is going to go well. More often than not, we're forced to endure and persevere in order to survive the day. In order for us to be the best we can be, we must learn how to endure and persevere. Life isn't going to sit back and let us have our way. We're constantly forced to make decisions and learn to manage what life has in store for us.

We're all faced with situations from time to time that push us to the limit that affect us directly or indirectly. As we try to balance personal ambitions and daily responsibilities, self, others, and worldly influences will stir up conflict, hinder our progress, attack our weaknesses, and create havoc on our emotions and intellect. But, we must learn to recognize these influences so we can balance daily responsibilities and personal ambitions. It's during these times, we can see the glimmer of God's work providing us with hope and encouragement to endure. Accept the trials that come your way as a way of strengthening your vulnerabilities so you can master the art of coping, applying yourself, developing the right attitude, and the art of "access denied" to negative influences and distractions. Take one day at a time. And, let these moments train you for the future.

No matter how difficult life gets, don't give up! Press on, remain hopeful, work through it, and believe this too shall pass!

Life is what you make it!

To everything there is a season, and a time
to every purpose under the heaven...
(Eccl. 3:1).

Every day we're faced with challenges and the unexpected. Not taking into account acts of nature that can cause havoc in one's life. Things happen, we can't control. Sometimes, our choices and the choices of others can cause us problems. We're all here on earth for a short time. So, why not enjoy the time we have. How you choose to use that time, is up to you. There is an art to living a fulfilling life personally, professionally, socially and spiritually. And, if you learn certain principles, there's no limit to what you can accomplish and the scope of your happiness!

If you want to enjoy life and achieve your goals, you must be willing to make the right choices and work for it. Human nature and outside influences will often get in the way and influence your thoughts causing you to make mistakes. Learning the hard way helps build character and teaches you a lesson. But, it's not a recommended way of learning. If you aspire to achieve and want the good life, you must be willing to follow sound advice, accept correction, and curb your thoughts and behavior. If you train yourself to make the right decisions on a regular basis, it will come naturally. And, you'll see the transformation occur in your life.

Each of us are born with certain innate abilities and skills. And, finding what skills and abilities we possess takes time. Earning a living doesn't have to be a chore you hate waking up to each day. It should be something you enjoy. After all, you'll be doing it every day so why not enjoy what you're doing so you can stay encouraged to grow in your craft.

Learning to manage your finances and credit wisely is also important. Prioritize your spending by focusing on what is needed. Filling up your closets and drawers with items you'll only wear or use occasionally is not a good use of spending your money. That money could be invested elsewhere or in other ways that are more profitable or beneficial. Create a monthly budget. Plan ahead. Learn to save. Develop good habits managing your money and credit so you can enjoy financial peace of mind.

Learn to build meaningful relationships with your family, friends and associates. You can't always help who you associate with so you must learn to manage those moments tactfully. Finding the right companion with whom you can grow and mature takes time. Your companion, friends and associates should be people you can trust, help you stay balanced, blend with your personality, and treat you with respect. Interact with people with whom you can build a positive relationship, share life's experiences and build a healthy social lifestyle.

It's important to balance work, social activities and relaxation. Learn to relax and enjoy peace and quiet from time to time. A good night sleep can help you wake up feeling refresh and alert. Or, take a day off to rest. People who learn to balance work, socialize and rest are the ones who achieve and perform at their best.

Make it a habit to enjoy clean entertainment and social activity. Learn to interact in positive ways with one another. Avoid unhealthy gatherings, heavy drinking, inappropriate behavior, casual sex, and negative influences. Travel and explore the world to learn about other cultures and lifestyles.

It's also important to establish a relationship with God. With God present in your life, you're better equipped to cope with the unexpected and life's experiences. God can make the good times better. And, the rough times seem not so rough. Get to know God and encourage Him to be active in your life and be willing to put into practice the insight and teaching He provides. Life can be beautiful. But, it's what you make it!

Accomplishing!

To everything there is a season, and a time
to every purpose under the heaven...
(Eccl. 3:1)

Personally learn to make the right decisions, balance work, socialize and rest.

Professionally find the right trade or profession that fits your personality and skills.

Socially learn to build healthy relationships and explore the world.

Spiritually build a relationship with God.

There's a season for every purpose in life. First, the decision. Deciding what needs to be done and how. Two, planting. Devoting time to carry out your decision. Three, harvesting. You begin to see the results of your efforts. And, lastly, the rewards. You accomplished your decision and can enjoy its benefits!

The Importance of REST, sandwich in between....

So the people rested. ...
(Exod. 16:30).

When you spend time working toward the fulfillment of your destiny, time off is a welcoming moment. There's nothing like kicking back and taking time to relax. Time off after you've completed an assignment, task or day's work allows you time to gather your thoughts, unwind and gain a sense of balance.

The peace of mind that comes from being still is priceless. The more you learn to rest, the more profitable you can be. Rest and quiet time does wonders for your well-being.

But, remember to rest and enjoy responsibility. Frivolous enjoyment can bring ruin and destruction. Find safe, enjoyable ways to entertain and have fun. Dine with a friend. Attend a movie or theater show. Spend an evening with family, friends or loved one. Plan a vacation. Honest, clean, safe enjoyment is refreshing.

Master the art of living and understand the importance of rest sandwich in between all you do!

The Good Life!

*And all these blessings shall come on thee,
and overtake thee, if thou shalt hearken
unto the voice of the Lord thy God
(Deut. 28:2).*

What is the Good Life? In Biblical terms, the "good life" is not defined by material wealth, fame, or worldly success but is deeply rooted in a relationship with God, living according to His will, and finding fulfillment in spiritual values. Here's a look at what constitutes the good life from a Biblical perspective:

1. A Relationship with God
- The foundation of a good life is a personal and meaningful connection with God.
- Knowing God personally and living in fellowship with Him leads to a life of ultimate purpose and satisfaction.

2. Righteousness and Holiness
- A good life is characterized by moral integrity and obedience to God's commandments.
- Living righteously involves justice, compassion, and humility before God.

3. Love and Service
- Loving God and loving others is central to a good life.
- A life of love leads to deep fulfillment and aligns with God's greatest commandments.

4. Contentment and Gratitude
- A good life is not about accumulating possessions but finding contentment in God's provision.
- Gratitude and trust in God bring inner peace and joy.

5. Peace and Joy
- True peace and joy comes from God and are not dependent on circumstances.

6. Purposeful Work and Stewardship
- The good life includes working diligently and being good stewards of what God has entrusted to us.
- Engaging in meaningful work honors God and contributes to human flourishing.

7. Eternal Perspective
- The good life is not confined to this world but focuses on eternal rewards and a heavenly inheritance.
- Living with an eternal perspective helps believers prioritize what truly matters.

8. Community and Fellowship
- A good life involves fellowship with other believers and mutual encouragement in faith.

The good life is a life lived in harmony with God's will, characterized by love, joy, peace, righteousness, and an eternal hope. It is a life of spiritual depth, relational harmony with God, man, and the world, purposeful work, and trust in God's sovereign plan. It is less about external circumstances and more about internal transformation through faith in Jesus Christ.

The Right Attitude!

The Spirit of God works best in our lives when we have:

Faith
- Believing in the fulfillment of things to come

Hope
- Convinced that God is working on our behalf for the fulfillment of our faith
- Lead by the spirit of our pursuit and not by the desires of our human nature

Love
- For God and others
- Inspiring us to act

Work
- Toward the fulfillment of our faith
- Exercising discipline and self-control

Patience
- Enduring trials calmly and without complaint

In this way, the Spirit of God can move on your behalf and assist in fulfilling your faith. Faith is believing in things hoped for. Having the right attitude is key to overcoming the challenges you face each day. The right attitude is a state of mind, a firm belief, a determination that enables you to endure opposition calmly and with patience. It's a freedom from things that trouble you. Developing the right attitude takes time and requires having a clear awareness of your situation and how to cope with it.

It's a guarantee our circumstances will not always be what they should be when trying to get things done. Everyday will not always go well. Human nature is sure to get in the way. The decisions we make. And, the decisions of others will directly or indirectly affect us. Unexplained events and circumstances will take place that will interfere with our commitment. These are all stepping stones used to bring you to maturity and strengthen your vulnerabilities.

Whatever the reason for your circumstance, be trained by it. Look past the moment. Look to the future. Make whatever changes are necessary. Do what is required. Let time take its course. Endure without complaining. Believing God is helping and enabling you along the way. By doing so, you'll be wiser, stronger, and better equipped to handle similar situations as life goes on. And, thankful you held the right attitude!

Make Each Day Count!

And God called the light Day, and the
darkness he called Night. And the evening
and the morning were the first day
(Gen. 1:5).

I remember the beginning of the year as if it were yesterday. Celebrating the holidays and enjoying time with family and friends. It was good to have time off.

Now, the holidays are over and we're back to the routine of life. Do you ever wonder if there's more to life than this? You go to work, come home, eat, tend to the family, relax, doodle around the house, watch TV, tend to household chores, run errands, and squeeze in some down time before turning in and starting the cycle over. During our younger years, time wasn't important. We had plenty of time to do as we please. And now that we're older and have more responsibility, we have less time for ourselves and things we would like to do. Time goes by so quickly. And, serves as reminder how precious each day is!

Suppose, you wanted to go back to school, pursue a new career, change jobs, start a hobby or business. How would you find time? Are you willing to make the necessary changes to your daily routine? Are you willing to cut back on leisure time and socializing to accomplish your goals? Are you willing to commit? Or, is it not the right time? By prioritizing and changing your way of thinking and habits, you can accomplish anything. Change is essential to accomplishing what needs to be done. After a while, we get into a daily routine that's hard to break.

We get lazy or lack motivation. We find excuses and put things off. Particularly, if it's something we don't like, is boring, difficult or requires a lot of time, we take a "wait and see" attitude or "I'll get to it later." The more you procrastinate, the harder it is to get started. Procrastination promotes a non-productive attitude that makes you anxious, impatient and frustrated whenever challenged. That frustration can spill over into your relationships, and other areas of your life and cause problems.

Often times, we're given insight into what needs to be done, how to do it and when. But, we find excuses not to follow through. Human nature and temptation will influence our decision causing doubt and test our sincerity about what we want to do. We must learn to manage these influences if we want to accomplish what needs to be done.

For the most part, there's enough time in a day to get done what needs to be done. By planning, changing your way of thinking, managing your time, disciplining yourself, sacrificing, organizing, prioritizing, compromising and working it out. You can accomplish anything, you're willing to do. You may have to sacrifice, give up some things, re-arrange your schedule, plan errands and activities differently, and restructure your social life. When you do this on a daily basis, life takes on a whole new meaning. And, frees your time to accomplish what needs to be done or some of the things you would like to do.

Your dreams, ambitions and desires are yours. So, you can't expect others to be as excited as you are about what you want to do. There may be times when you won't have the cooperation or encouragement of others. But, you have to stand your ground and be willing to do whatever it takes with or without their cooperation. You can't satisfy everyone. Or, be involved in so many things, you can't get anything done. Sometimes, you have to say "no" and work your way through it.

At times, things will take longer than expected. Responsibilities, commitments and life in general will interfere with your plans. Things happen, life is an evolving process. That's why it's important to maintain a daily relationship with God to help you manage "life". There is an art to living! And, God can equip you with whatever you need. With God's leadership and support, you can accomplish anything. It doesn't mean, it will be easy. It will require sacrifice, commitment and effort on your part. But in the end, it's worth it. So, "*Just do it!*"

It's a Balancing Act!

Let me be weighed in an even balance,
that God may know mine integrity.
(Job 31:6)

If you're planning to start a business, pursue a degree, certification, or some ambition that inspires you, you must learn to balance your time between pursuing your ambition, personal responsibilities, and loved ones.

While pursuing your ambition, you can't abandon your loved ones. By the same token, you need to devote as much time as needed to accomplishing what needs to be done. And, hopefully, your loved ones will understand and allow you the freedom and peace of mind to focus on your pursuit. If not, talk to them about it. Try to work it out. Once you accomplished your goal, it may afford you more pay, a better job, more confidence and other opportunities you didn't have before.

It will take time, sacrifice, and discipline to overcome the challenges of pursuing your ambition and balancing your time between personal responsibilities and loved ones. Set achievable goals daily. Plan ahead. But, take it one day at a time. Create a to-do-list for what needs to be done today, tomorrow, in a week and a month from now. Stick to the schedule as best you can. Make adjustments as needed along the way for responsibilities and the unexpected. As you meet your daily, weekly and monthly goals set aside time to spend with your loved one, family or quiet time to yourself.

Some days you'll accomplish more than expected. And, other days might not go as planned. Stick to it. Push yourself. Step out of your comfort zone. Be flexible and don't box yourself in with old habits and routines. Don't waste time. It's a balancing act to get done what needs to be done!

Be Yourself!

*Happy is the man that findeth wisdom, and
the man that getteth understanding
(Prov. 3:13).*

Be yourself...

1. Don't rush into things.
2. Take your time.
3. Set priorities.
4. Use your time wisely.
5. Work toward the fulfillment of your faith.
6. Exercise patience and endure trials calmly.
7. Develop the right attitude.
8. Have faith lead by the spirit of your pursuit and not by the desires of your human nature.
9. Hope for things to come.
10. Pray for what you need.
11. Find balance between work, rest and enjoyment.
12. Strive to develop SELF.......

  S- Strive to do your best daily.
  E - Encourage Godly living.
  L - Live one day at a time.
  F - Form healthy relationships.

Emotions

... Blessed are the pure in heart (Mat. 5:8).

Emotions play an active role in your daily living. Emotions are a physical, conscious expression of your inner being reacting to life experiences. So, it's important that you learn to master your emotions to help you cope with life's experiences, build character, enjoy relationships and inspire you to achieve.

During periods of emotional highs and lows, your inner being or voice is aroused and wants to cry out and express itself. That expression invokes feelings or emotions. And, if not managed properly can open the door to all sorts of problems. It's difficult to use sound judgment when you have mixed emotions. Likewise, it's not good to substitute emotion when intellect is needed. Examine your circumstances, reflect on your relationships, see what you've learned, and make whatever changes are necessary so you can manage your emotions.

We're all human! And, can be devastated by events that take place in our life. But, be mindful of your reaction. It can make matters worse. Sometimes, it's best to walk away and gather your thoughts before reacting to a situation or deciding what to say. Give yourself time to settle down and gather your thoughts. Be careful what you say and how you say it so you can have a clear conscience and not be troubled by guilt or regret later. Say as little as possible to make your point. Too much talk or even rehashing the same thing over and over can open the door to negative dialogue and make matters worse. Something said out of meanness, anger or violence can affect your well-being.

Emotions are a powerful part of human nature that can help us build character, inspire us to achieve and enjoy life's experiences. Take time to understand your emotions. So, you can live life with feeling!

Guard your emotions....

*And, the peace of God, which passeth all
understanding, shall keep your hearts and minds...
(Philip. 4:7).*

We all want to be happy and enjoy the good life. One of the keys to enjoying life is to control your emotions. When you're happy, you feel good. When you're unhappy, you're distressed and uneasy. Emotions are a vital part of your living experience.

We all get caught up in an emotional moment from time to time. We can't help it. Our environment, circumstances, interactions and relationships with family, friends, associates and strangers can all affect us emotionally. When your emotions are aroused, if you don't learn to manage and express your emotions properly, it can lead to regret, sorrow and cause more harm than good to yourself and others. Even, a joyful moment can turn sour in a blink of an eye if you're not careful. You must learn to use your mental facilities to help regulate your emotions. And, learn not to substitute emotion when intellect is needed. Sometime, it's best to wait until you had a chance to calm down and think before reacting. Once said, you can't take it back. Your apology maybe accepted. But, the damage may be done.

So, it's important to be mindful of what you say and how you say it. Fill your heart with good things and guard your emotions so you can cope with life's experiences, build character, enjoy relationships and enjoy life!

Mom!

*Train up a child in the way he should go: and
when he is old, he will not depart from it
(Proverbs 22:6).*

By Melanie Prather, my wife

On my birthday in the year of the Lord, Mom gave birth to me. In my mom's womb, my faith journey began. Every week she would read the Bible to me. And when I came into the world, Mom continued reading the Bible to me. From birth, she instilled in me the fundamental principle of "love" for God and my neighbor.

There's a special love that exist between a mother and daughter.

My mom is someone who loves and is not afraid to show love. My mom sometimes pushed aside her needs to focus on the needs of her family.
My mom is a listening ear when no one else would listen or care. My mom would give advice when asked. But, always with the understanding that it's only advice, leaving me free to make my own decisions.

Though at times, mom and I disagree. She would respect my decisions.

So, MOTHER.....

M is for the many things you shared and gave to me.
O means you're only growing wiser.

T is for the tears you shed while raising me.
H is for your heart, full of love.
E is for your eyes, glowing with love for God.
R means right you'll always be.

But to me, you're "Mom"!

Father

But now ye also put off all these; anger, wrath, malice, blasphemy, "filthy communication out of your mouth. Lie not one to another, seeing that ye have put off the old man with his deeds; and have put on the new man, which is renewed in knowledge after the image of him that created him (Colossians 3:8-10).

F – Faithful
A – Acceptable
T – Trustworthy
H – Honorable
E – Ethical
R – Respected

Faithful. Men, be faithful and loyal to your companion and children.

Acceptable. Be a welcoming site to your companion and children.

Trustworthy. Be someone your companion and children can trust.

Honorable. Be honest, not corrupt, evil or ill-mannered.

Ethical. Be up-right in character, maintain a good sense of values and principles.

Respected. Be a person admired for your abilities, qualities and character.

Men love your companion. Remember, women wasn't taken from the head or foot of man but from his rib. Nor, was women created to be superior or subordinate to man. But, instead, to be his companion side by side as a support system for one another serving different roles working together in love as one.

Men are to be examples for your children, not by word. But, by sight. Your words have meaning. But, your actions tell all. Let your words coincide with your actions. In this way, you will teach your children and they will not depart from it.

Christian Love!

And now abideth faith, hope, love, these
three; but the greatest of these is love...
(1 Corin. 13:13).

You may be able to speak many languages. But, if there is no love in your speech, your speech is a clanging bell. You may have the gift of inspired preaching; know and understand many things; and even have faith that can move mountains. But if you have no love in your heart you're an empty shell. You may give away everything you own to charity. But if you have no love for your fellowman, you're of little value.

Love is faithful, patient and kind. It's not jealous, conceded, proud, ill mannered, selfish or irritable. It does not seek to destroy, hurt or neglect others. Nor, does it keep record of wrongdoing.

What good is it to say "I love you", if you show no love. Your words and deeds should be a reflection of God's love which will be made clear in the light of heaven.

Be a conduit of God's love growing in faith, hope and love. Faith rest in the hope of things to come. And, in the presence of love, faith is blessed with the love of God!

Companionship

Submit yourselves to one another
(Eph. 5:21).

Life is beautiful when you've found the right companion to enjoy life with. Someone who compliments your personality, helps you to grow and mature, rounds out your rough edges, and brings balance into your life. Finding the right person takes time and doesn't happen overnight. Compromise, sacrifice, and working things out all play a role in making a relationship work. It's not a one-sided arrangement. Each of you are unique and have your own way of doing things. At times, you may disagree. It's okay. It's healthy! But come to a mutual understanding regarding your disagreement and compromise for the sake of the other.

When you're in a relationship, it's not about you it's about your mate. Your body is not your body. It's your mate's. It's not about what you want but what's best for both of you. This requires compromise, sacrifice, patience, self-control, suffering, endurance, and emotions that require balancing. It's all about sharing, growing, and experiencing life together in such a way it adds dimension to your being.

Forming the right relationship with the right person takes time and can help build a healthy lifestyle. Your companion should help you grow as an individual, providing friendship and companionship. There are many reasons why a man and woman are drawn together. Once the euphoria of intimacy settles, reality sets in and the business of learning about one another begins. A companion should understand your interests, giving you time and space to grow and accomplish what needs to be done. Intimacy helps you to connect emotionally and satisfies a human desire.

Intimacy can also cloud your judgment. It should be postponed for as long as possible, until you've had a chance to know the person and their associations. Forming a relationship involves taking on the person's family, friends, associates, and lifestyle. So it's good to know what you're getting into before proceeding any further. Many relationships have ended unpleasantly or with an unwanted pregnancy because of premature sex and lust.

Dating, if done wisely, can help you learn as much as you can about your companion and minimize the chance of ending up in a bad relationship, or even worse, divorce. It should tell you about the person's likes and dislikes, family background, personal aspirations, hobbies, religious interest, sexual interest, spending habits, smoking, drinking, sleeping, hygiene, and more.

Knowing which personality traits are tolerable and which are not is key to longevity in a relationship. If any of the traits bother you, weight the pros and cons. It may be tolerable now but what about later? Months or years from now, when your patience have run thin dealing with the same thing over and over? Take time to know the person. And keep alive the physical, mental, and spiritual connection that brought you together so you can remain in love a long time!

Affliction!

Behold, "I will bring it health and cure, and
I will cure them, and will reveal unto them
the abundance of peace and truth
(Jer. 33:6).

Throughout life, we all will be afflicted with sickness at one time or another. Even, if you eat right, exercise and take care of your body you're still susceptible to illness. If you're not taking care of yourself illness can be self-imposed through poor eating, lack of exercise, poor health management and not getting checked regularly by a doctor. Even, poor dental hygiene if left unchecked can lead to serious health problems. Illnesses, such as cancer, show very little signs in the early stages. But, if left unchecked can lead to serious health problems. So, it's important to get your vaccines, have your blood tested and see a physician and dentist on a regular basis for early detection of signs and symptoms that can lead to health problems.

In general, illness is a state of not feeling well and its cause has to be identified or determined in order to find a cure or recover. Illness can stem from many causes such as pathological, psychological, physiological, genetic, environmental, lifestyle factors, lack of physical activity, substance abuse, chronic stress, social and economic factors, unsafe working or living conditions, immunological, allergic reactions, hypersensitivity to foods or environment, developmental causes, abnormal prenatal development due to maternal health or exposure to substance, idiopathic, iatrogenic illness or injury caused by medical treatment or procedures such as side effects of medications, surgical errors, behavioral and reckless activities, aging and degenerative, infectious agents beyond viruses, bacteria, fungi, parasites, trauma or mechanical physical injuries, burns or fractures from accidents or violence, nutritional deficiency to name a few. So, without proper check-ups it's hard to determine what could be wrong when you're not feeling well. Whether its genetics or not, affliction can happen any time.

God has given us incredible abilities to endure and overcome affliction. Our body is equipment with defense mechanisms that are triggered when foreign bodies invade our system. With proper treatment and support from God, family, friends and loved ones we can overcome affliction. And, feel better soon!

A Healthier You

*Beloved, I wish above all things that thou mayest
prosper and be in health, even as thy soul prospereth
(3 John 1:2).*

We enjoy eating. It's a favorite pastime. It's a pleasant way to enjoy time with family, friends, or relax at home. After a long day at work there's little motivation for cooking a big meal. We have chores to complete, work to do, studying, homework, and other things to attend before we can rest and go to bed. With our busy lifestyle, the microwave has become a popular appliance for preparing and heating meals. And the weekend holds more chores to complete, errands to run, activities to attend, a night out, food on the go, all affect our ability to eat healthy and exercise.

Without proper diet and exercise, your body becomes burdened with unwanted substances that can speed the aging process and lead to tooth decay, obesity, high blood pressure, heart disease, cancer, and more. Disregarding genetic influences, the majority of our health issues originate from our eating habits, drinking, smoking, and lack of exercise. Selecting the right foods and eating the right portions can provide your body with the nutrients needed to function properly, minimize the need for vitamin and mineral supplements, and reduce the effects of food sensitivity. You can also help maintain your ideal weight by finding foods that are healthy, filling and low in calories without the harmful ingredients and side effects.

Fasting from time to time can help you control your eating.

There are many benefits to fasting. It helps discipline your will and gives your body a break from the constant digestion of solid food. Occasional absence from solid foods and drinking plenty of water can flush out unwanted substances and aid your body's rejuvenation process. Proper eating, fasting, and regular exercise can improve your relationships, combat stress, increase your mental acuity, slow the aging process, and help you stay fit physically, mentally, and spiritually.

Some of us would like to exercise, but time constraints, responsibilities, lack of motivation, cost, and availability of fitness centers are some of the reasons why we don't. If you're wanting to exercise, see how you can adjust your schedule to develop an exercise routine that fits your lifestyle, such as bicycling, jogging, walking, swimming, treadmills, or aerobics to help rid your body of unwanted substances, build stamina, improve your cardiovascular and pulmonary system, and shed unwanted pounds. A cardiovascular workout can help you to feel young again and full of energy.

Your local library or bookstore has several books, magazines, and videos you can use to help design an exercise routine that's right for you. You can also find lots of information on the internet. Don't overexert yourself when you first start. Take it slow. Give yourself time to get into a routine and find what works. Pushing too hard at first can create injury and discourage you from continuing. Choose a plan that fits your lifestyle. What works for others, may not work for you. So, please, consult your doctor or a trained professional before engaging in any kind of diet or fitness program. Make the commitment. And get started in creating a healthier you!

Fasting!

*And, when he had fasted forty days and
nights, he was afterward and hungred. And,
when the tempter came to him...
(Matt 4:2-3).*

Fasting is a good form of discipline over our most basic human function – eating! For the most part, none of us are missing any meals. We're snacking and eating regularly throughout the day. Or, we eat light during the day. And, fill-up when we get home. As a result, our body is not given a chance to properly digest the food. So every time we eat, we get sluggish or sleepy until our body has consumed the food and found its balance. Constant eating can cause us to be overweight and create all sorts of health issues. By fasting on a regular basis, we can manage our health.

Fasting is abstinence or going without food, drink or both for a period of time. The ideal fasting period is twenty four hours. The best fasting period is twelve to fourteen hours. However, a person may fast for days. Or, any length of time he or she chooses. For example; breakfast is the breaking of a fasting period. Usually, it takes three to five hours to digest a meal depending upon what you eat and how much you eat. If you drink water during the fasting period, it can flush your body of unwanted waste and byproducts. Fasting can also be used to help manage your weight. Dieting is not the same as fasting. Dieting is a way of managing what and how much you eat. It is not abstinence from eating.

Fasting is used in the healthcare profession, before and after certain procedures and treatments. It's also observed by many religious sects. And, has been used to make a political statement to promote awareness and change. Mastering your eating habits can help you develop the self-discipline needed to succeed in other areas of your life.

In addition to the physical benefits, fasting can also provide some psychological ones as well. It's a way of training your mind to make changes. Because of the physical and physiological changes associated with fasting, I suggest you consult your doctor before fasting. When fasting, take note of how your body is reacting to going without food or drink. And, its effect on your ability to focus. When your body is depleted of a function or habit it has become a custom to, it will begin to command your attention and send all sorts of signals both physical and psychological. Managing these signals is key to learning the art of discipline and self-control.

During the fasting period, we're vulnerable to temptation. Jesus was tempted periodically throughout His forty days and forty nights of fasting. Temptation doesn't appear when we're strong and able to resist its influences. It only appears when we're vulnerable and susceptible to them. Temptation uses whatever appeals to us, to influence us. So, it's important we recognize the influences of temptation while fasting.

Fasting is a wonderful way to learn and master the art of living!

Are you ready to get fit?

For they are life unto those that find
them, and health to all their flesh
(Prov. 4:22).

Perhaps this is a good time to think about getting fit. In today's fast pace lifestyle, it's easy to forget about our health. Good times with family and friends, planned vacations, eating out, and little exercise can lead to unpleasant results at the doctor's office. Exercise and diet is a good way to maintain your health, stay fit, live long and prosper.

When it comes to exercising at the gym or home both provide pros and cons. Some people prefer to get out of the house and go to the gym. The change in scenery can be encouraging and refreshing. On the other hand, the gym has many distractions that can interfere with your concentration and time spent exercising. And, if you're only able to get to the gym a few times a month the cost of joining should be considered.

On the other hand, exercising in the comfort of your home can be a convenience. You can throw on an exercise outfit and not worry how you look. If you use a treadmill, jog or walk, it's an easy way to stay fit around the house. There's little temptation to socialize. You're not busy watching others, listening to conversations or easily distracted. You can focus on your exercise, save time on travel and cost. And, even squeeze it in between work you have to do at home. It's an inexpensive, convenient way to stay fit. However, the confinement of your home or surroundings can be discouraging and hinder your enthusiasm.

Whether you exercise at home. Or, at the gym. It's a win either way. Decide which exercise routine is best for you, add variety to your workout and you'll be motivated to stay fit.

It's also good to eat balance meals of fruits, vegetables, carbohydrates and meats. Drink plenty of water. And, eat in moderation to maintain your energy level and stay alert. Often times, we eat more than we should and get sleepy. This slows us down, makes us sluggish and lazy. And, interferes with our ability to concentrate and get things done.

Eat healthy, exercise, see a doctor and dentist regularly will help you maintain your health and feel good about yourself!

A Request for Help!

*And I say unto you, Ask, and it shall be
given you; seek, and ye shall find; knock,
and it shall be opened unto you*
(Luke 11:9).

Life has a way of putting us in situations that require us to seek help. No one has all the answers and knowing who can help, can be difficult. Who can I trust? Who can I ask? Who can help? Will they hold me in debt to them if I ask for help? Will they want something in return? Do I ask a family member, friend or associate? These are some of the questions we ask our self when trying to find help and get answers. Sometimes, our pride keeps us from seeking help when we need it. But, more often than not, we're hesitant to seek help because of the uncertainty.

Although, it's hard to know who to ask for help. There is one who is always willing to help. And, that is God! God is always willing to be a part of our life and help when needed. All you have to do is, ASK! For most of us, God is our last resort when all else fails. If we go to God first, He'll let you know who you can trust and ask. He'll move about on your behalf opening doors, moving people to act in your favor, find solutions and bring about resolution. But, if you go to Him last. You may have limited your options. Or, made matters worse. By seeking God first, He can tell you what you need to know to solve the problem. Or, send you someone who can help. God welcomes the opportunity to get involved in your life and move on your behalf. When you show a willingness to acknowledge and accept God's intervention, it helps you build a relationship with Him. We all face decisions and situations beyond our control. And, we're not always going to know how to react or what to do. But it's comforting to know, God knows what to do and how to help. Even, if He is the last resort, He's always willing to be a part of our daily living experience.

You may not see what God has done to make possible your request for help. He may have influence someone to act in your favor, prevented a situation from getting worst, given you something you needed, saved you from or prevented an accident, made you late only to find out why later. God works in so many ways to help us daily. You can't see the how. But, you can see the results. You asked, He answered! When God has answered your request, thank Him personally for what He has done. Acknowledging God's participation in your life, will open His heart to helping you more. In this way, you can build a relationship with God. And all you need do, is "Ask"!

The Limits of God!

Thy will be done, as in heaven, so in earth
(Luke 11:2).

God can do many things. But, He's limited in what he can do! He can heal your body. Cure your sickness. But, it's up to you to see a doctor and take your medicine. He can help you pass an exam. But, He can't make you study. He can help you with your finances. But, you have to manage the money.

God can help you in many ways. He can lead, encourage, inspire, influence and even alter outcomes on your behalf. But, you have to do your part for His efforts to work. God can help you in your personal and profession life. But, He can't do the work for you. That's something He has left up to you. The most difficult task or impossible situation can be overcome, if YOU carry out what is required of you. God speaks to us in many ways when He wants to help. He'll speak to you personally, through others and even arouse your consciousness to give you insight and answers. And, depending upon the situation will intervene on your behalf whether you ask or not. God wants to be actively involved in your daily living experience and not just an innocent bystander. When you interact and commune with Him in positive ways. He moves and acts on your behalf. It's amazing what He can do!

So, I encourage you TODAY! Seek God in all you do! And, do what God says. Do the work. Put in the time. Remain faithful to your commitment. Be patient. And before long, you'll be receiving the reward and benefits of your efforts. God can do many things. But, it's all up to YOU!

God is waiting to hear from you!

*Hitherto have ye asked nothing in my name: ask
and ye shall receive, that your joy may be full...
(John 16:24).*

Ask, and it will be given; seek, and you will find; knock, and it will be open. God is always willing to be a part of our life. And, help when needed. Sure, God will act on your behalf at times without your asking. But He has left when to help, up to you.

If someone is always meddling and helping you whether you want it or not, after a while you'll get annoyed and maybe even angry. Our parents have tried many times to help us in any way they can whether we ask or not only to meet resistance. How are we to learn, if someone is always thinking and doing for us?

When we exercise our free will and ask for help it gives the person permission to get involved in our life. Until the person has our acceptance and cooperation to get involved, the person is limited to what he or she can do. Whether it's a parent, friend, neighbor or God, when we ask for help we can see the person's willingness to get involved and your acceptance of their involvement. Your acceptance is key to moving mountains.

God in His infinite wisdom realized this, so He decided to leave it up to you when you want Him involved in your life. It's through prayer, you can ask God to get involved in your life. Or, the life of someone else. This allows Him to do things He couldn't do until you gave Him permission. When you ask God to intervene in the life of someone else, He's still limited to what He can do.

Because, He was not given permission from the person who needs it. Our relationship with God is individual and personal. Each of us has to form our own relationship with God to truly benefit from His involvement. God will still act on your behalf for someone else as a way of forming a relationship with that person and help build the relationship with the person who made the request. This serves as a witness to strengthen your relationship with God and opens the door for God to form a new relationship with the person on your behalf.

The potential of going before God and making your request known has unlimited possibilities. Many unexplained wonders have been performed through our petitions to God. We have the power to overcome obstacles, perform miracles and accomplish anything just by asking!

How Do I Pray?

When thou prayest, thou shalt not be as the hypocrites. But, when thou prayest, enter into thy closet, and when thou hast shut thy door, pray to thy Father in secret; But when ye pray, use not vain repetitions, as the heathen do: for they think that they shall be heard for their much speaking (Matt. 6:5–7).

Prayer is our way of personally communicating with God and forming a relationship with Him. When your prayer is answered, it's evidence He exist. The more you rely on God, the closer your relationship becomes with Him. So, it's important you learn how to pray.

God is spirit! So, you must commune with God in spirit. When you pray, go to a quiet place and verbally express yourself to God the Father, in the name of Jesus, with a sincere heart, clear conscience, and genuine belief that your request will be answered without using a lot of meaningless words or giving a false impression. Whether you call upon God from the privacy of your home or during a crisis at the spur of the moment, you should have a certain level of confidence your request will be answered and God can help. If you have faith the size of a mustard seed, you can say to this mountain move and it shall move, and nothing shall be impossible for you. *(Matt 17:20-21).*

Prayer should come from your inner being or spirit and not from rambling thoughts or words that come to mind. Learn to allow your spirit to speak with the Spirit of God. When you're troubled, your inner being cries out. When you're happy, it wants to express joy. So, it's important to learn to let your inner being speak, whether you're happy, troubled, or at peace. In this way, you will invoke the Spirit of God to act on your behalf.

We all need help in some form or another from time to time. And, sharing our innermost feelings to ask for help can make us feel vulnerable and uncomfortable. Particularly, if we're not sure how the person will react. Or, if he or she can help. Or, know how to help can deter us from asking for help when needed. This is not the case with God. God can help, wants to help and be a part of your life. All you need do is ask. It's also important you say "Thank you, God" when your request has been answered.

How do I thank God? You can thank God in many ways for what He has done in your life. Start with a sincere "Thanks you, God", tell someone what God has done for you, help someone in return, attend a worship service and express your gratitude for His help, add extra dollars to the collection plate or donate to charity as a way of acknowledging God has supplied your need. There are many ways to say "thank you" to God. God wants to be a part of your life. All you have to do is pray!

My New Year's Prayer

By Melanie Prather, my wife

Thank you, thank you, God!

Heavenly Father, as I begin a new year, I thank you for taking me through the past year. I know I could not have made it without your love and protection. When I think about all the blessings in my life, I cannot help but rejoice and say thank you!

Thank you, God, for your loving presence in my life. You have provided me with all I need to live happily and successfully.

Thank you, God, for my family and friends. So many people have blessed my life that I am honored by the privilege of sharing their acquaintance.

Thank you, God, for a place to call home, a place where I can be myself. A place where I can feel safe and secure, surrounded by love.

Thank you, thank you, God, for all the blessings in my life! I am so grateful to be a part of you and your worldwide family! Lord, you are everything to me.

Continue to help me rejoice daily, pray without ceasing, and give thanks in all circumstances. This is your will! Lord, I ask this in the name of your Son, my Lord and Savior Jesus Christ. Amen.

Fruitful Living!

*The thief (adversary, sin) cometh to steal, kill,
and destroy: I (Jesus) come that they (man)
might have life, and have it more abundantly
(John 10:10).*

Give thanks to God daily.
- God helps us in ways seen and unseen.

Master your thoughts.
- Rid yourself of thoughts that interfere with your well-being.
- Sow seeds of joy and encouragement.

Rid yourself of:
- Pride, Anger, Gluttony, Lust, Envy, Greed, and Laziness.
- These will frustrate you and rob you of your joy.

Learn to be grateful with what you have.
- We all have what we need to be happy.

Strive to do your best.
- Requires a commitment.
- A commitment to:
  - Learning.
  - Accepting correction.
  - A willingness to change.
  - Doing what is required.

Don't rush time.
- Each day is precious.
- Learn to use your time wisely.
- Set priorities.
- Find time to work, rest and enjoy.

Develop joy.
- Joy produces happiness.
- Happiness cultivates success.

Love yourself and others.
- Develop in the fruits of the spirit – love, joy, peace, longsuffering, gentleness and faith.
- Love is kind and patient.

Consider yourself fortunate when faced with adversity and challenged.
- Adversity, hardship, difficult situations are steppingstones toward maturity.

Praise the Lord your God with all your heart.
- Commune with God.
- Read your Bible.
- Make note of answered prayer and what God has done for you.
- Give thanks.
- And, Worship!

In this way, you'll be blessed!

Keys to Daily Living!

I call heaven and earth to record this day
against you, that I have set before you life and
death, blessing and cursing: therefore choose
life, that both thou and thy seed may live.
(Deut. 30:19)

Learn a Profession or Trade.
   Plan ahead.
   Work for something with all your wisdom, knowledge, and
skill.

Strive to do your best.
   Learn to be satisfied with what you have.
   Be grateful and enjoy the fruits of your labor.
   Be thankful for every day you are alive.
   Do not let worry cause you sickness.

Love one another.
   Love your neighbor as yourself.
   Love God with all your heart, mind, body, and soul.
   Two are better off than one.
   Husband and wife shall love one another and become one.

Enjoy life.
   Make the most of each day.
   Strive to do your best daily.
   Time is precious, don't waste it.
   Be glad when things are going well and when trouble comes.
   Live joyfully with the one you love and others.
   Have reverence for GOD and obey his commands.

A Tree of Life!

In that I command thee this day to love the Lord thy
God, to walk in his ways, and to keep his commands
and his statutes and his judgments, that thou may
it live and multiply; and the Lord thy God shall bless
thee in the land where thou shall go to possess.
(Deut 30:16)

We should inspire to be a tree of life. Upright in character, rooted in the Word and nourished by the love of God.

Throughout the Bible and history, we learn our talents are gifts from God. Given to us at birth. And through proper nurturing from our parents, friends, associates and life in general, we can discover our talents and put them to use to earn a living, provide for loved ones, and benefit others. There are many people with exceptional talent that were able to accomplish great things and acquire great wealth. Imagine how much more fulfilled and successful they might have been if they had cultivated a relationship with God while developing and utilizing their talents. When we allow God to nurture the gifts He has given us, we gain a deeper understanding of success and fulfillment.

By allowing God to be a part of our life, it can transform our life. God, who created us, desires to be part of our lives and tries to communicate with us in various ways—through the stirring of our inner spirit or guidance from others. By being open to His influence, we can make wise decisions and live comfortably. However, this requires us to listen, follow advice, and accept correction. When guided by our inner spirit, strengthened by discipline and self-control, we can overcome worldly distractions and harmful human tendencies which can lead us astray or to our demise. By embracing God's influence, we develop qualities like love, joy, peace, patience, kindness, goodness, faithfulness, gentleness, and self-control, which help us resist destructive influences and align our lives with God's purpose.

On the contrary, sin and wrongdoing can diminish our talents. History shows us many examples of gifted individuals whose abilities and achievements were undermined by public exposure of their sins. Their wealth, influence, and opportunities were lost as a result of their actions.

Those who rely on worldly ways and our human abilities, it will get us but so far. And, if you're not careful those same influences can lead to your downfall. Human nature, with its tendencies toward pride, greed, envy, deceit, and other destructive behaviors, often leads to strife, rebellion, and suffering. The seven deadly sins—pride, deceit, violence, wicked schemes, eagerness to do wrong, stirring up conflict, and falsehood— illustrate how if left unchecked worldly influences and human nature can lead to ruin. Without the guidance of God's spirit, we risk falling victim to these harmful tendencies.

When human nature dominates our life, it can interfere with our harmony between man, the world, and God. If we take away or suppress the spiritual element of our existence, we're reduced to relying on our human (physical and intellectual) nature to make decisions and navigate through life, missing key elements essential to living a fulfilling and satisfying life. These key elements allows God to work through us, in us, and with us, nourishing our inner being and sustaining our physical self. Those who learn to balance their spiritual self and human nature are transformed into the individuals God created us to be, exemplifying true success.

When things are going well, we're happy and have a peace of mind. However, when things are not, how we manage those moments can bring us peace or unrest. Having a clear perception can help us make decisions and navigate life difficulties more effectively. We as people should be constantly evolving into the person we were born to be. Like a tree of life, we should draw strength from the soil (the Word of God) which nurtures and nourishes the roots (our inner being, soul or spirit) and sustains the tree (our physical or cardinal being) allowing us to bear fruit. In this way, we can be transformed into the person God intended us to be, living a life of purpose, fulfillment, and harmony!

Why do I need God?

For God so loved the world, that he gave his only begotten Son, that whosoever believeth in him should not perish, but have everlasting life (John 3:16).

God existed before anything else, including time as we know it. He is self-sustaining, self-sufficient, all-knowing, and all-powerful. God lacks nothing and needs nothing. Yet, in His infinite wisdom, He chose to make Himself known. Over time, humanity came into being. With our first breath, we received a small part of God's essence and His splendor. God, in His foresight, knew what challenges we would face. So he devised a plan, so we could experience and know Him, enjoy a relationship with Him, and receive the blessings of having Him actively involved in our lives while navigating through life. Not for His sake, but for ours.

It is written that if you love the Lord your God with all your heart, mind, body, and soul, and love your neighbor as yourself, you will reap great rewards. By incorporating these two commandments into your daily life, you can be transformed. God helps everyone, whether they realize it or not, whether they believe in Him or not. He is always present. Once you truly know and experience God, it's an undeniable feeling that cannot be explained—only experienced. While you cannot see or physically touch God, you can hear His voice, witness His works, and sense His presence. The more you know Him, the more you'll appreciate Him and see His impact in your life.

It's possible to live a good life without acknowledging God because He has given us free will to choose. So why, then, would someone need God if they can manage without Him?

With God in your life, you gain the strength to cope with life's challenges. God provides counsel, correction, hope, support, protection, and so much more if you allow Him to be active in your life. He desires for you to enjoy life, be happy, and reach your full potential. Each of us is uniquely made, and our individuality was given at birth, along with the breath of life that made us living souls.

Our souls connect us to God and give life to our physical bodies. Without spiritual influence, life is often governed solely by our physical senses, intellect, emotions, and the world around us. This is the life of a non-believer, one who has little or no relationship with God. But when you allow your spiritual self to influence your life, you gain a deeper understanding and ability to commune with God. This helps you navigate life beyond what your physical senses or intellect alone can manage.

Think of moments when an inner voice urged you: "Don't do that," "Stay away," or "Be cautious." That quiet prompting isn't mere instinct—it's the Spirit of God communicating with your soul, guiding you in ways your physical senses cannot. God sees what you cannot: the intentions of others, potential dangers, or the right path forward.

Unlike instinct, which is shared by both humans and animals, the ability to commune with God is unique to humanity. When you invite your spiritual being to guide your life, you gain clarity, wisdom, and a more fulfilling existence.

Your existence here on earth is for a short time, and God desires for you to live it in harmony—with others, the world, and with Him. That's why you need God: to ensure your time here is filled with purpose, joy, and the richness that comes from His presence in your life.

I'll be damn!

*Having damnation, because they
have cast off their first faith
(1 Tim. 5:12).*

Since humanity is naturally inclined toward sin and often lives apart from God, salvation is the only way to escape the consequences of sin and a life without Him. Salvation represents deliverance from sin and its consequences, encompassing both personal commitment and divine intervention. By choosing to let God into your life and cultivating a relationship with Him, you embark on the process of renewal—what is often called being "born again." This personal decision is yours alone to make; no one can make it for you. Mere acceptance of salvation is not enough—it requires change. If your life remains unchanged after accepting God, the consequences of sin will persist. Similarly, simply being a "good person" is not sufficient to save you; your thoughts, words, and actions can still lead to condemnation.

Salvation is a twofold process. First, it involves accepting Jesus Christ as your Lord and Savior. In doing so, you acknowledge Jesus as the Son of God, born of the Virgin Mary, who lived among humanity, was crucified, died, was buried, and resurrected. After His resurrection, Jesus walked among people for a time before ascending to sit at the right hand of God, where He intercedes on behalf of humanity. This acceptance grants forgiveness for all sins—past, present, and future—and allows you to start anew with God as part of your life.

The second part of salvation involves transformation: changing your thoughts, behaviors, and actions to align with God's guidance. This is not about becoming "holier than thou"; rather, it's about equipping yourself to navigate life's challenges and grow into the person God created you to be.

Integral to salvation is the concept of redemption—the process of freeing yourself from the consequences of sin by making the necessary changes to live according to God's teachings. This isn't an easy task, especially if it requires you to alter longstanding habits or relationships. Change is often difficult, but any changes God asks you to make are ultimately for your benefit. Just as parents' guide their children for their good, God's direction is rooted in love and wisdom, even when the reasons aren't immediately clear.

Salvation is a free gift. No amount of good deeds, moral behavior, or religious activity can earn it. It is offered to everyone, regardless of background or circumstance. Whether you are moral, religious, immoral, or nonreligious, all are judged by the same standard of God. Why, then, should you pursue salvation if it cannot be earned? Because God has made a promise: those who accept His Son, Jesus, will be forgiven and saved from eternal separation from Him. This promise marks the beginning of redemption, a journey where you take responsibility for your actions and strive to live in alignment with God's will.

Throughout life, God offers guidance, protection, discipline, and empowerment to help you thrive personally, professionally, socially, and spiritually. With God's help, you can achieve far more than you could relying solely on your own abilities. But you must be willing to embrace redemption and take the steps needed to turn away from wrongdoing.

At the end of life—on Judgment Day—your soul will enter eternity. While earth is the dwelling place of your physical existence, your soul's eternal home will be either heaven or hell. God has provided clear instructions for salvation, for living a fulfilling life, and for joining Him in heaven. These instructions are universal, applying to all people regardless of race, color, or creed. There is one rule for all.

The next time you say or hear the phrase "I'll be damn", consider what it means, a soul condemned for their sins. Salvation offers the only path to escape that fate and live in the eternal presence of God.

Life's Journey— Fulfilling My Purpose

*And he said, Let us take our journey, and
let us go, and I will go before thee
(Gen 33:12).*

There is an art to living a satisfying life personally, professionally, socially, and spiritually! It requires understanding your potential, tapping into your strengths and utilizing your abilities to learn, grow and mature. Life has a way of alerting us to what we must do to be complete as a person. Often times, we ignore the signs. Sometimes external influences can affect our ability to perform, steer us off course, and rob us temporarily of our happiness and rewards. But, by learning to master these influences, you can fulfill your destiny and live a fulfilling life.

Life is a journey to be experienced one day at a time. A journey filled with emotional highs and lows, challenges, and setbacks that can produce personal growth and well-being. It takes determination, know-how, and the ability to overcome obstacles. It requires taking on responsibility, making sacrifices, planning, organizing, and coordinating your efforts toward personal freedom and growth. And not let distractions move you hastily away from your objectives. Master the art of "letting go" and put the past behind you means to stop dwelling on negative experiences or emotions from the past and choose to focus on the present moment, accepting what happened without letting it control your current thoughts and actions. In essence, it's about moving forward without being held back by past events. When in doubt, listen to your "inner voice." Go slowly, have faith, plan, and organize.

There is an art to living. It requires developing the right attitude, associating with the right people, building the right relationships, and exercising good judgement through learning, experiencing, and working things out. Success doesn't happen by chance. It comes in stages by successfully carrying out your plans. Remaining focused, believing, and working toward the fulfillment of your purpose.

In the Day of Your Power

But truly I am full of power by the spirit of the Lord
(Mic. 3:8).

In the day of your power, you will be transformed into a new person and break strongholds! As you develop in character and take on the fruits of the spirit, God's anointing will enable you to perform at a higher level. God will move and act on your behalf, influencing others to help you along the way. There will be growing pains as you grow in awareness through study and applying life teachings. Worldly influences and others will distract and hinder your pursuit. Unexplained events and circumstances will take place to challenge your commitment. Human nature will also get in the way. By learning to recognize worldly influences, distractions, unexplained events and circumstances, and the influence of human nature you can master life's challenges and improve your chances of success.

God wants you to have a good life, walking in His will, achieving your full potential. For this reason, have reverence for God so he may strengthen you and enable you to do exceedingly well.

You're empowered!

*..the anointing which ye have received from him
abides in you, and ye need not any man teach
you: But as the same anointing teacheth you
all things, and is truth, and is no lie, and just
as it hath taught you, ye shall abide in him
(1John 2:27).*

We all have the ability of accomplishing anything we put our mind to. Unfortunately, we can only accomplish so much. But, with God's help we can accomplish so much more. Difficult and challenging situations don't seem as stressful when God is involved. As you grow in your relationship with God and put into practice His teachings and principles, you become anointed and empowered to perform at a higher level. God's anointing works in two ways. First, is the inward flow which occurs when God's spirit connects with your spirit or soul enabling and empowering you to perform above and beyond your own capabilities. The second, is the outward flow which occurs when the Spirit of God empowers and influences others to move and act on your behalf.

As you strive to perform at your best, people and circumstances become an active part of your life. People are the platform by which you learn to be all that you can be personally, professionally, socially and spiritually. Striving for excellence means doing your best each day. You can be successful without a relationship with God. But, your success is limited. Your abilities are limited. Your resources are limited. Your options are limited. Everything is limited to your own natural and physical abilities.

It's humanly impossible for you to live a well-rounded satisfying life without God. Man is a two dimensional being – physical and spiritual. The spiritual side can only be satisfied with a relationship with God. Without it, you're a one dimensional being.

When God is pleased with your life and your relationship with Him, He anoints you and empowers you with His abilities and wisdom. As you grow closer to Him, you begin to receive His gifts and shed your human nature. Accomplishing this, is not easy. First, you must be willing to develop spiritually and mentally. The adversary will unexpectedly catch you off guard and use whatever influences necessary to cause you to falter. Human nature your five senses, emotions, intellect and physical body will also try to influence your thoughts, decisions and behavior. From time to time during your period of growth, God's empowerment will fade when worldly influences and human nature take over.

Those who make an effort to include God in their life get to experience life in a different way. It's a life that can only be experienced. Your choice to include God is not forced upon you. But, given freely if you choose. One of God's greatest gifts to mankind is the freedom of choice and free will. No other living creature walking, flying or crawling has the freedom of free will. God wants to be a part of your life and wants you to have a good life in every way possible. With His participation, there is no limit to what you can accomplish when you're empowered!

Why Church?

For where two or three are gathered together in
my name, there am I in the midst of them...
(Matt.18:20).

Imagine a world where all Christian services, in the United States and across the globe, worship on the same day, lifting their voices in praise and honor to God. Such unity would not only leave a profound impact on individuals but surely bring joy to God. The mission work being carried out today to spread the gospel is truly remarkable. People are reaching out to local communities and distant nations, sharing the Word of God just as Jesus commanded—to go into all the world and proclaim the good news.

It's hard to fathom what it must have been like for the twelve disciples to see Jesus face to face each day, witnessing His miraculous signs and wonders and hearing His words of wisdom. They must have been in awe of His teachings, even if they couldn't fully comprehend them at the time. How blessed are we to believe in Him without seeing Him with our own eyes? The miracles and wonders that Jesus continues to perform today affirm that He is alive. Through faith, we see His work, receive His grace and mercy, and are united as members of the Church of God—a family of believers.

Why is attending church important? In this context, "church" refers to Christian religious services. Is church meant for socializing, fellowship, or worship? Or does it serve a deeper purpose? The Sabbath—a day set aside for rest and worship—

was established for believers to gather publicly and give honor and praise to Jesus Christ, our Lord and Savior. The central message of the Bible is the coming and fulfillment of a Savior for humanity. In the Old Testament, God revealed Himself to mankind and provided a way for people to seek salvation. However, it became clear that humanity could not achieve salvation on its own. In His infinite wisdom, God made a way in the New Testament by sending His Son, Jesus, to bear our sins, offering salvation to all who believe in Him. God has given Jesus dominion over this world, the universe, and the heavenly realm, while God Himself oversees all creation, both physical and spiritual. At its core, the church is all about Jesus.

Unfortunately, some places of worship are plagued by lengthy services, discord, backbiting, power struggles, and contradictions to biblical teachings. These issues can discourage believers and lead to declining attendance. A believer's attitude toward the church often reflects their faith. Faithful Christians attend church regardless of the actions or attitudes of the congregation. Those with mixed feelings about their pastor or fellow worshippers may attend sporadically, while others may stop attending altogether, impacting their faith and spiritual growth. Every congregation has its own unique personality, philosophy, and teachings. It's crucial to find a church that aligns with your personal and spiritual needs, one that encourages regular worship and growth.

Listening to sermons on the radio or television and studying the Bible are valuable, but they cannot replace the personal experience of gathering with other believers. Worshipping together, hearing testimonies of God's work in others' lives, and receiving God's message in person can transform your own life.

Church attendance is a universal Christian responsibility. Unless you are sick, disabled, or have unavoidable obligations, you are called to attend. In countries like the United States, where religious freedom allows open worship, this responsibility is a privilege. However, in some parts of the world, practicing Christianity openly can be life-threatening. Church should be a place where believers work together in unity and respect while promoting God's Word. By adhering to biblical principles, the church can maintain its sanctity and unity.

Over time, the concept of church has grown to include morning services, Sunday school, Bible studies, mission work, and various ministries. Yet the essence of church is not the building—it is the gathering of believers. It is a space for fellowship, communion, worship, and spiritual growth. Above all, it is a place to honor and worship our Lord and Savior, Jesus Christ.

You've got soul!

*And the Lord God formed man of the dust of
the ground, and breathed into his nostrils, the
breathe of life; and man became a living soul
(Gen. 2:7).*

You've got soul! And, without it, your body would be a lifeless mass of tissue and bone (physical body). Your soul is "life" which entered your body when you took your first breathe at birth. It was then you were brought into existence and made aware you are "a living being". Your physical body is a dwelling place for your soul or inner being. The soul contains the breathe of life or spirit of man that connects you to the Spirit of God and allows you to commune with Him. It is this connection that bonds us to God.

When your physical body comes to an end, your soul or inner being will leave your body and transition into the spiritual realm where it will live forever. Just as birth is the beginning of life. Death is the beginning of life eternal, a place for your soul to reside.

Where do we go from here?

For we know that if "our earthly house of
this tabernacle were dissolved, we have
a building of God, an house not made
with hands, eternal in the heavens
(2 Cor. 5:1).

With all the tragedy that's taking place in the United States and around the world; I thought it would be a good time to mention about our departure from this earth. Unless a love one or someone close to you is dying or has died, you don't give it much thought.

A time will come when your life here on earth will come to an end. Somewhere in the spiritual realm, there's a place for your soul or inner being. A place where there is no life or death. Your physical body will return to "the ground" from whence it came. And your soul will be released and transition into the spiritual realm where it will spend eternity. During that transition, you'll have a moment to look back and meet God!

And, when you reach the gate of heaven, Jesus or His appointed Angel will greet you to determine your fate of eternal existence. It doesn't matter what's your religious belief, Jesus will be the one to determine your fate. He'll answer the question He has asked you so many times "Do you know me?"

If you allowed God to be part of your life and tried to live according to His teachings and principles, He'll answers "yes". And, welcome you home into His heavenly realm where your soul can enjoy freedom from life in this physical world and its influences. A place where your soul can enjoy peace of mind that comes from being in the presence of Jesus, His angels and all His glory. A place where your soul can live forever in peace.

But, if you lived your life in accordance to your own desires and influences of this world free from any relationship with God, your soul or inner being will spent its life enduring eternal unrest. Your soul will be denied access into heaven and sent to a place unlike heaven and earth. A place where evil governs. And, God is not present. A place of torment and suffering, filled with evil creatures and all the ungodly elements of this world. A place where there is no rest or peace for the human soul, a place called "Hell".

The mystery that surrounds the creation of the worlds, universes, mankind and all living things were set in motion "in the beginning, God created...." And, for those of you who have decided to know God and make Him a part of your life will get to meet Him face to face, give Him a hug and say; "Thank you, I'm glad to be home!"

Welcome Home!

*And Jesus went out, and his disciples, into the
towns of Caesarea Philippi: and he asked his
disciples, saying unto them, Who do men say I am?
(Mark 8:27)*

There are many spiritual beings that exist throughout the heavens and earth. And there are various beliefs about God, who he is, and what he represents. But, we should only be concerned with the one true God - God the Father, and God the Son, Jesus Christ. In the beginning, God created the heavens and the earth. And for a short time, He took on human form in the name of Jesus (the Son of God) and walked among us spreading the gospel of His existence and teaching us the art of living. Jesus was crucified at the hands of humans for mankind sake. And, was buried. On the third day, Jesus awakened from death and dwelt among us again for a short time, confirming His existence and who he is. Then, He returned home filled with the fullness of God the Father ruling the heavens and earth with justice, power, and might. The Trinity of God - The Father, the Son, and the Holy Spirit.

If you travel around the world or observed the scenery in movies, you may have noticed the beauty and wonder of this creation. When you sit at an airport and observe the different nationalities, have you noticed what a beautiful race of human beings God has created? And, when you watch nature shows and see all the different kinds of creatures that can live in some of the harshest places on earth where temperatures are below zero, above 100, or in volcanic ruins, places where humans cannot live. When you see the creatures that live in the air, seas, and walk the earth, you can't help but be amazed at what God has created. It was prefect from day one and is still perfect today. God's presence is everywhere (omnipresent), helping us in ways seen and unseen, moving about on our behalf, serving us with unconditional love, hoping that one day you get to know Him, and can join Him in heaven, look Him in the eye, and say, "Thank you. It's good to be home!"

You can order Creating a New You online at:

Amazon.com

BarnesandNoble.com

Or, other online bookstores.

To order by phone, call the author or your local bookstore.

Merchants can order by calling Ingram.

www.ingramcontent.com/pod-product-compliance
Lightning Source LLC
Chambersburg PA
CBHW031220120626
46545CB00003B/926